Serenity's Dealing *With* Divorce - God's Guidance

Written By

Timsha R. Batiste

Illustrated by

B.Huzaifah

Serenity's Prayer

God, grant me

the Serenity to

accept the things

I cannot change,

Courage to change

the things I can,

and the Wisdom to

know the

difference.

For permission requests, write to the author,

addressed " Attention: Permissions" as

info@batistestories.com

Timsha@dreamtodayllc.com

Timsha R. Batiste

Houston, Texas

www.batistestories.com

www.dreamtodayllc.com

Ordering Information:

"My Hair Power"- Hardback ISBN: 978-1-7360761-0-1

Ebook ISBN: 978-1-7360761-1-8

Paperback ISBN: 978-1-7360761-2-5

"Dominique's Healthy Choices"- Hardback ISBN: 978-1-7360761-4-9

Paperback ISBN: 978-1-7360761-3-2

Ebook ISBN: 978-1-7360761-5-6

"Mommy, What Time Is It?"- Paperback ISBN: 978-1-7360761-6-3

Ebook ISBN- 978-1-7360761-7-0

Available On: Amazon, Lulu, and Ingramsparks

Printed in the United Statesof America

Acknowledgment

All praises to my Heavenly Father for allowing me to bring to life children's books. My hope is that this book will make a great impact on a child's life.

Serenity, you have changed my life and you have been a great inspiration to me. Sweetie, you have inspired me to be better, ever since the day you were born. Thank you for being such a God given blessing to me. I hope to continue to write more children's books that will inspire you as you grow older. I will always love you!

Mama- Thanks for Loving me!

Cassandra Stallings- Thanks for your listening ear, love, concern, and support in everything I do!

Eleanor Jackson- Thanks for your support and being such a great person!

Shenna Bradley- Thanks for inspiring me and being my friend!

Gregory Banks- You have made my life better while going through a very tough time. Thank you for listening, praying, helping, caring, and supporting me in all that I do.

A. Mansion- Thanks for your support!

Erika B- Thanks for your prayers and encouragement

Tammy Harris- Thanks for your prayers, support, and encouragement!

Shareen Addison- Thank you for your prayers and encouragment!

To all of my family and friends who always support me, thank you! I Love You All!!!

Dedication:

This book is for every child who has dealt with the hurt of a Divorce. Remember life is not over and know that it wasn't your fault.

"Mommy and Daddy are separating."

That's what they told little Serenity.

"Mommy and Daddy are getting a divorce".

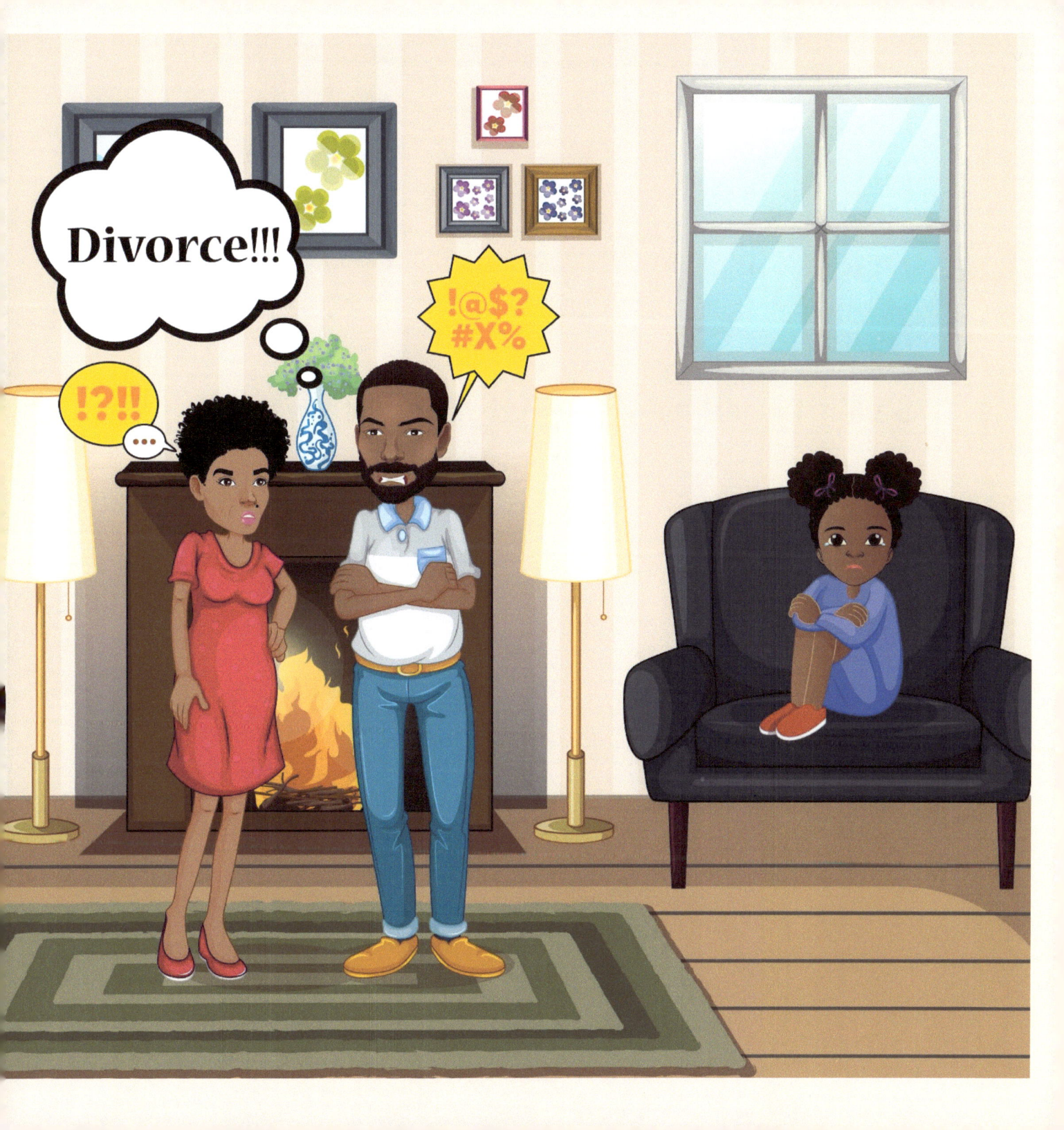

Serenity had no idea what a divorce was but she knew it wasn't good.

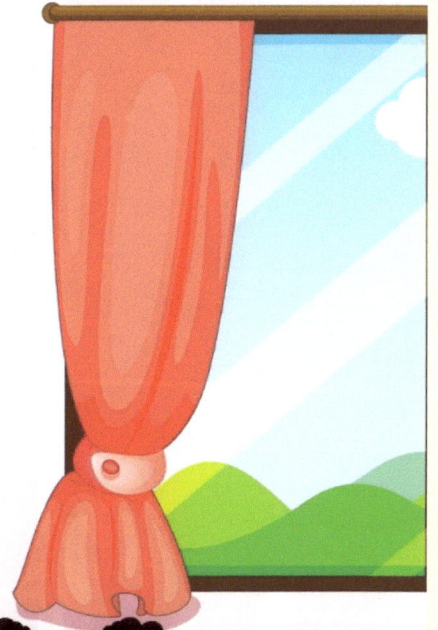

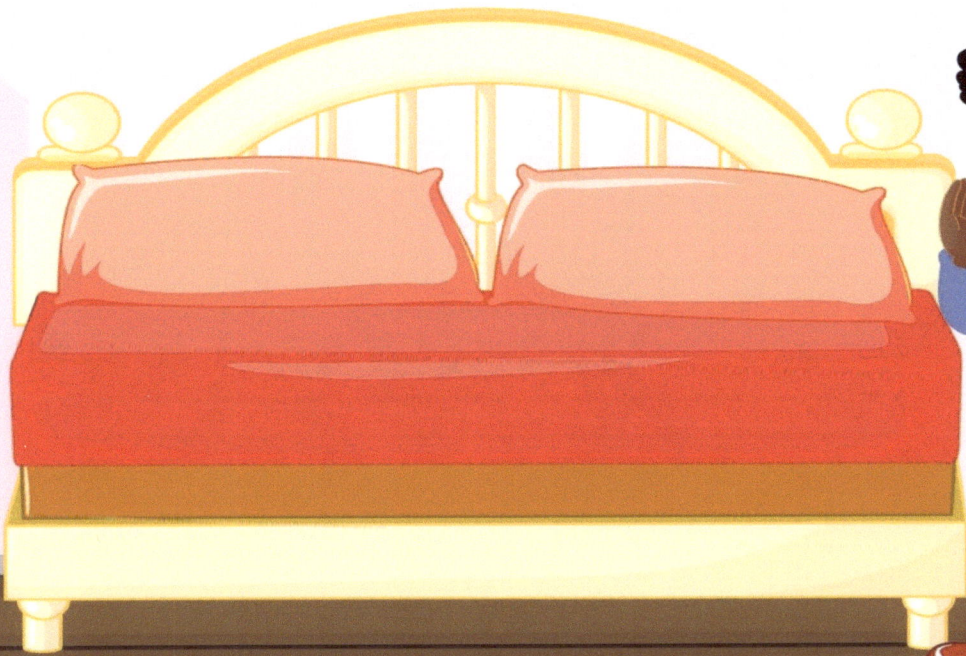

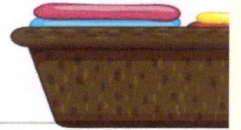

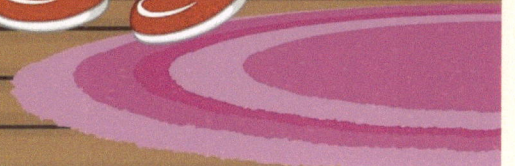

Serenity was so confused.

Had she done something wrong? Was this all her fault? Could she put a stop to it?

After a week, Mommy and Daddy started sleeping in different rooms.

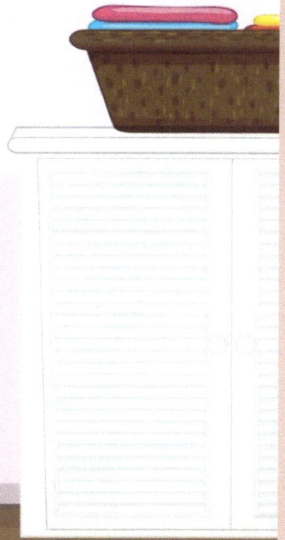

After two weeks, Daddy moved out into his own apartment.

After three weeks, Daddy didn't visit the house much anymore.

After a month Serenity's Dad filed for a Divorce.

Serenity would be living with Mommy and would only see her Dad every other weekend.

That made her cry. Serenity would get sad just at the thought of her Dad not being at home. She was used to seeing her Dad every single day. Now she had to wait 14 whole days between hugs.

Serenity loved her parents so much but, no matter how much she loved them and how much she tried, she couldn't bring them back together.

Most nights, Serenity would sit up on her bed and pray for Mommy and Daddy to get back together.

She would pray for Daddy to move back home.

She would pray for them to love each other again.

But every morning she would wake up and nothing had changed.

Serenity's little heart was broken.

But as time passed by, she realized it was not her fault.

Mommy and Daddy had separated because of arguments and her dad no longer wanted to be a family.

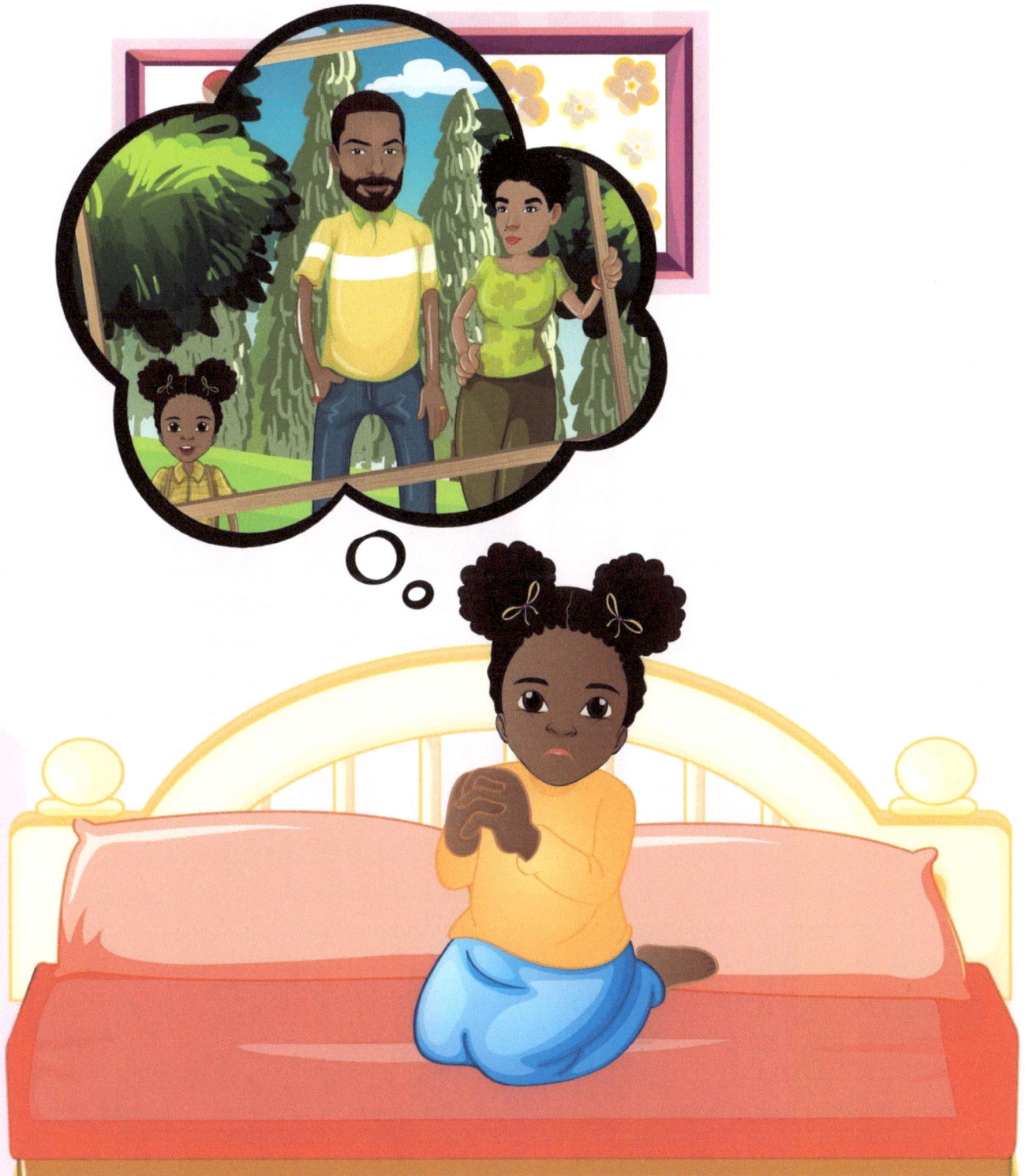

Serenity would get upset when her Mommy and Daddy had arguments.

" Daddy, Mommy don't want to argue". Serenity said

Sometimes her Mommy would cry during arguments and Serenity would be their to console her.

Serenity only wanted her parents to be loving and happy.

Serenity's Mom would have talks to help her understand what was happening.

Soon, she stopped praying for them to love each other again. Instead, she only prayed for them to be happy, and God answered those prayers.

With the love and guidance of God, Serenity managed to make it through those tough times. Even though there is a long road ahead, God will continue to see Serenity through.

Mommy and Daddy still loved her. And she loved her Mommy and Daddy. That was all that mattered.

The End

www.ingramcontent.com/pod-product-compliance
Lightning Source LLC
LaVergne TN
LVHW072100070426
835508LV00002B/196